MONUMENTAL INSCRIP

ST. ANDREWS KIR~~~~~~
Parish of St. Andrews-Lhanbryde
Morayshire

and

BLACKHILLS
Near Lhanbryde
Parish of Elgin, Morayshire.

Compiled by
Members of the Moray and Banff Branch
of the
ANESFHS

Edited by
Bruce B. Bishop FSA Scot.

No part of this publication may be reproduced, stored in a retrieval system or transmitted in any form or by any means electronic, mechanical, photocopying microfilming, recording or otherwise, without the prior permission of Aberdeen & North-East Scotland Family History Society

Copyright 2002 Aberdeen and North-East Scotland Family History Society

ISBN 1-900173-53-0
First Published December 2002

Published by
Aberdeen and North-East Scotland Family History Society

Printed by
Rainbow Enterprises, Howe Moss Crescent, Kirkhill Industrial Estate, Dyce,
Aberdeen

INTRODUCTION

This booklet contains transcriptions of the Monumental Inscriptions in the now disused burial ground associated with the church of St Andrew, formerly the parish church prior to the amalgamation of the parishes of St Andrews and Longbride in 1782. The original church was burned down in 1727: "*August the 6th day 1727. The Church of St Andrew with all the seats therin was burnt to Ashes by a boy shooting Doves sitting thereon...*". (*National Archives of Scotland CH2/317 St Andrews Kirk Session Minutes*). The church was rebuilt by 1733, and was finally demolished in 1796, but traces of the outline can still be identified as ridges in the grass.

The burial place is surrounded by a stone wall and occupies rising ground on the west bank of the River Lossie. The early plans of the burial ground indicate that it contained a large number of enclosures, but only one of these, the Leuchars Aisle, remains intact (and now totally inaccessible).

The numbering sequence used in this publication has followed that used by the Manpower Services Commission index, as this is already held on computer at the Local Heritage Centre, Grant Lodge, Elgin. Due to the fact that the tombstones are not arranged in rows, as is common in most burial grounds, the original survey appears to have used a spiral numbering system.

The plans for the burial ground have been redrawn in October 2002, to show all stones in place at that date, and also the sites of some stones which have now been removed. It is noted by Shaw in his "*History of the Province of Moray, Volume 1*" dated 1882 that "a number of the gravestones were used to floor the kitchen of the Schoolmaster's house".

The index contains all surnames, even when used as a middle name, as these could indicate the surnames of parents or grandparents. Transcriptions are 'as read', and punctuation has only been edited where required in order to avoid misinterpretation.

The booklet also contains a transcription of the inscription on the single tombstone at the private burial ground at Blackhills House, originally the home of a branch of the Innes family, now owned by the Christie family. Although Blackhills is actually in the parish of Elgin, due to its proximity to Lhanbryde it seems more logical to include it with the latter parish.

ACKNOWLEDGEMENTS

The Society wishes to thank all concerned in the preparation of this index. The recording was carried out by several members of the Moray and Banff branch of the Aberdeen and North East Scotland Family History Society. The editing, indexing and graveyard plans are the work of Bruce Bishop.

Special thanks are due to Mr John Christie for his kind permission for our visit to the private burial ground at Blackhills House.

Thanks are also due to Jean Shirer for her comments on the original draft of this booklet.

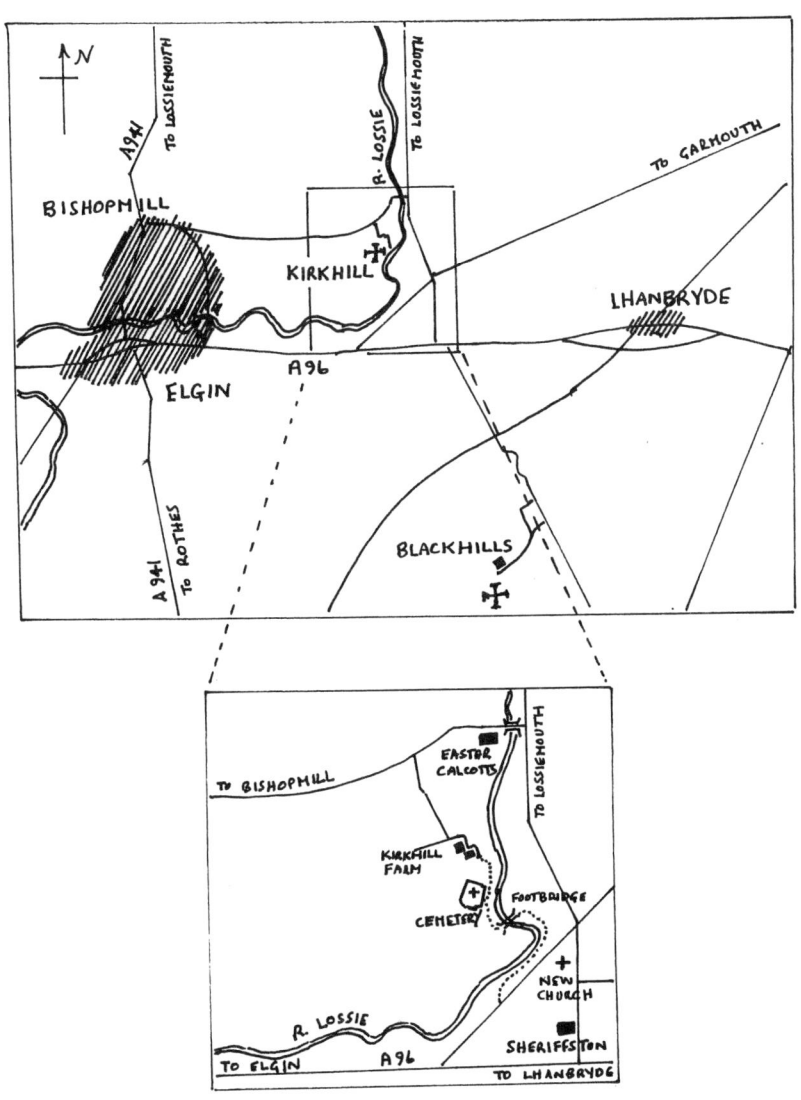

Location of the Burial Grounds

CONTENTS

Introduction   page iii

Acknowledgements   page iv

Location of Burial Grounds   page v

Monumental Inscriptions, Kirkhill   page 1

Monumental Inscriptions, Blackhills   page 12

Index   page 13

Plan of Burial Ground at Kirkhill 2002   page 15

Plan of Burial Ground at Kirkhill
showing earlier enclosures and pathways   page 16

MONUMENTAL INSCRIPTIONS

KIRKHILL CHURCHYARD

PARISH OF ST ANDREWS – LHANBRYDE

1. Sacred to the memory of MARGARET McDONALD the dearly beloved wife of JOHN BENNETT who died at Woodside of Leuchars on 3rd April 1879 aged 30. R.I.P. Also the said JOHN BENNETT who died at Aberdeen on 3rd Novr 1907 aged 69.

2. In loving memory of JOHN FRASER who died at Calcots 18th April 1894 aged 63 years, also his wife ANNE INNES who died at Elgin 23rd March 1922 aged 84. Their son HENRY FRASER who died 6th October 1926 aged 60 years and his wife CATHERINE MARGARET BARNET who died 5th June 1953 aged 72 years.

3. *Stone no longer in existence.*

4. Erected by ANGUS NICHOLSON to the memory of his dearly beloved wife JANE ANN ANDERSON, born at Woodpark, St Andrews, Lhanbryde 1st July 1849, died at Glasgow 9th Feby 1891. Also in loving memory of the said ANGUS NICHOLSON, who died at Kingussie 6th March 1919 in his 71st year. "A light unto my path".

5. The Dunbar-Brander Enclosure.

5a. In loving memory of ELSIE, 2nd daughter of F.E. THOMPSON of Marlborough and wife of A.A. DUNBAR-BRANDER, Imperial Forest Service, India. Married 1st Novr 1902 and died at Pachmarhi, India 22nd May 1803. "Thy will be done". And of the above ARCHIBALD A DUNBAR-BRANDER born 23rd April 1877, died 31st March 1953. And of his second wife FRANCES EMILY who died 10th April 1954.

5b. Sacred to the memory of JAMES BRANDER DUNBAR-BRANDER of Pitgaveny. J.P. and D.L.Co. Elgin.
Late Captain in the Scots Greys, formerly Lieut. in 3rd Light Cavalry, Madras, Adjt. of Governor's Bodyguard, son of Sir ARCHIBALD DUNBAR of Northfield, Fifth Bart., by his 2nd wife MARY, daughter of JOHN BRANDER of Pitgaveny, born 6th January 1825, died at Pitgaveny 16th November 1902. "My presence shall go with thee and I will give thee rest". Of ALICE GRANT his wife, died 6th December 1936.

5c. To memory of JAMES BRANDER DUNBAR of Pitgaveny, late Captain Queens Own Cameron Highlanders, and also Kings African Rifles, J.P., D.L. Moray. Elder son of JAMES DUNBAR-BRANDER, born 10th October 1875, died at Pitgaveny 25th December 1969.

6. The Paterson Enclosure.

6a. In memory of our dear father and mother, GEORGE PATERSON who died 20th Jan (19)52 aged 81 years, and of his wife ANNABELLA MORGAN who died 17th Sept (19)55 aged 84 years. Also their son THOMAS who died at Elgin 13th Jan (19)70 aged 60 years.

6b. Loving memory of my beloved husband and our dear father ALEXANDER MORGAN PATERSON Died 9th Sept (19)69, also his wife JANET HAY LEGGE died 14th Dec 1997. "Much Loved".

6c. *Masons Block.*
C.P.

7. Sacred to the memory of the beloved children of ROBERT and ELIZABETH STEPHEN, Schoolhouse:
JOHN ANDERSON, born 13th Feb 1878 died 5th June 1878. WILLIAM SELLAR born 14th March 1891 died 14th Sept 1900 at Longhill, Urquhart. Also of the Rev. ROBERT STEPHEN, M.A., for 39 years Schoolmaster of this parish who died 17th May 1910 aged 66 years and ELIZABETH CRANNA his widow who died at Elgin 24th April 1924 aged 74 years. Also ANN MARGARET, 4th daughter of the above who died at Aberdeen 9th March 1944 aged 59 years, also ROBERT who died at Elgin 5th March 1956 aged 79 years. Also their grandson Rev. Dr. JAMES SOUTER STEPHEN who died at Elgin 29th April 1997 aged 86 years, beloved husband of MAY KEITH JAMIESON. "Suffer the little children to come unto me".

8. Erected in memory of ALEXANDER LAMB, Farmer in Elgin, who died 25th March 1816 aged 86 years, and CHRISTIAN HAY his spouse who died 5th Sep. 1788 agd 47 & there (*sic*) son JAMES who died 2nd May 1792 agd 22 & MARGARET who died 24th March 1765 agd 3 years.

9. Erected by MARGARET GRANT in memory of her husband JAMES McDONALD who died 21st Novr 1868 aged 64 years. Their son JAMES died 16th Octr 1874 aged 32.

10. In loving memory of ELIZABETH DUNCAN, wife of GEORGE McARTHUR, Moss of Barmuckity, who died 16th July 1879 aged 52 and their sons PETER who died in infancy and GEORGE who died 24th Novr 1888 aged 29 years and is interred in Elgin Cemetery, and the said GEORGE McARTHUR who died 28th Augt 1902 aged 70 years.

11. Erected by JAMES HENDRY in memory of his children JAMES who died 31st Augt 1850 aged 4 years, ISABELLA died 28th Sept 1856 aged 6 years, MARY died 30th September 1856 aged 4 years, BARBARA died at Sheriffston 1st July 1864 aged 7 years. Also his wife ISABELLA McKENZIE who died 22nd Novr 1880 aged 60 years. Also his wife MARGARET PRIEST, died 27th Jan 1895 aged 72 years. Also the said JAMES HENDRY died 9th Jan 1901 aged 80 years.

12. *Stone no longer in existence.*

13. To the memory of JAMES WRIGHT, late ship owner in Banff, born 1767 died 1856, ELIZABETH ANDERSON his wife born 1777 died 1862. PENELOPE their daughter, widow of the late JOHN SMITH, baker, Aberdeen, born 1802 died 1865. ARCHIBALD DUNBAR, their son, 23 years Parochial Teacher, Rothes, born 1823 died 1865. LETITIA MARY, their daughter, born 1800 died 1866. MARGARET, their daughter, widow of the late WILLIAM MITCHELL, born 1800 died 1872. ELIZABETH, their daughter, born 1807 died 1886.

14. *Broken Stone*
1878. Erected by JAMES CAMERON, Carpenter, Calcots, and MARGARET CHALMERS his wife in memory of their children:
JAMES who died 13 January 1873 aged 21 months. PETER CHALMERS who died 30 April 1877 aged 11 months, and ALEXANDER who died 21 July 1883 aged 6 months. WILLIAM C. CAMERON who died 11 January 1905 aged 25 years. JAMES died 1 December 1912 aged 31. The above JAMES CAMERON died 12 March 1915 aged 72. His wife MARGARET CHALMERS died 2 October 1917 aged 78.

15. This stone is erected by ALEXANDER LEAL, Tailor in Longhill, in memory of his children who died in noneage.

16. *Masons Block*
W. TORRANCE.

17. *Stone no longer in existence.*

18. JOHN FALCONER, Manufacturer in Elgin. 16th October 1810 aged 49 years.

19. Erected by ALEXANDER McDONALD in memory of his children. MARGARET who died 26th March 1862 aged 2 years. MARY who died 30th March 1862 aged 5 years. JOHN who died August 22nd 1869 aged 3 years and 5 months. Also the said ALEXANDER McDONALD, who died at Moss of Barmuckity 15th January 1916 aged 82 years. Also his wife MARGARET FARQUHAR who died at Moss of Barmuckity 1st August 1917 aged 82 years and their son ALEXANDER McDONALD who died at Macduff 9th September 1938 aged 79 years. Also their son ROBERT of Melbourne who died 3rd September 1947 aged 92 years, buried at sea whilst returning to Scotland.

20. Erected to the memory of the Revd. JOHN WALKER M.A., who was minister of this parish for 26 years. Born 4 May 1816 died 8 Jan 1866. And of his children ALEXANDER GEORGE born 15 Nov 1842 died 24 Aug 1843, KATHERINE MARJORY born 14 Jan 1841 died 5 July 1849. CHARLES EMILIUS GORDON born 24 June 1844 died 19 Dec 1866. HENRY WILLIAM born 26 Dec 1854 died 23 Nov 1888 at Tuticorin, India. ROBERT

DUFF born 15 June 1848 died 29 Dec 1888 at Sydney, Australia. JOHN born 4 Dec 1847 died 10 Sept 1892 at Springfield, Tasmania. And of ANNE DUFF, widow of the said Revd. JOHN WALKER, and daughter of Major ROBERT DUFF of Ladyhill, Elgin, born 6 Aug 1817, died at Elgin 16 Sept 1896. ELIZA KATHERINE born 20 Dec 1849, died 25 Sept 1925, widow of HUGH ALEXANDER DUFF of Kereru, New Zealand, and last surviving child of the Revd. JOHN WALKER.

21. 1881. Erected by JOHN McLEAN, Farmer, Scotston-Hill, in memory of his beloved wife MARY JOHNSTON, who died 24th October 1870 aged 59 years, also his daughter ANN MacLEAN who died 21st September 1873 aged 19 years. The said JOHN McLEAN died at Scotston-Hill 24th Dec 1882 aged 60 years. Also of their daughter MARY, who died at Reed City, U.S.A. November 25th 1895.
N.B. two different spellings of surname on tombstone.

22. Erected in memory of BARBARA GILZEAN, wife of WILLIAM PETRIE, Farmer, St. Andrews, born 16th June 1817, died 4th October 1874, and of their daughter ELIZABETH, born 23rd July 1853, died 15th January 1876. Also the said WILLIAM PETRIE, died 13th March 1891 aged 80 years. Also of their daughter BARBARA born 19th March 1845 died 6th July 1901. Also their sons and daughters WILLIAM ASHER, died 29th June 1909, MARY ANN, died 26th November 1924, ALEXANDER, died 16th June 1927, HENRIETTA, died 26th April 1932, MARGARET, died 28th April 1832.

23. Erected by ISABELLA FERGUSON in loving memory and of your charity pray for the souls of my father WM SIMPSON who died at Longhill 26th April 1877 aged 67 years, my mother ANNIE SIMPSON who died at Longhill 13th Feby 1899 aged 86 years. My husband JOHN FERGUSON who died at Kiltycloghee, Co. Fermanagh, 11th Novr 1902 aged 60 years. Also my sons HENRY ALEXANDER, who died at Longhill 24th June 1901 aged 27 years, PATRICK CHARLES who died at Longhill 26th March 1906 aged 24 years. My daughter LUCY ANNIE who died at Longhill 15th Nov 1908 aged 32 years. Also of the above ISABELLA FERGUSON who died at Longhill 16th Feb 1933 aged 85 years.

24. CONSTANCE EVELYN DUNCAN.

24a. In loving memory of BRIDGET MARY MacKENZIE, died 4th Dec 1966 aged 88 and her sister NORA ISABELLA FERGUSON died 3rd May 1978 aged 98.

25. In memory of JAMES FRASER Esquire, late Farmer in Darkland, who was born 29th March 1802 and died 19th August 1873. Also of JANE LESLIE his widow who died at Darkland on 10th April 1880 aged 77 years. Erected by his sorrowing widow JANE LESLIE.

26. *Obelisk with top broken off*
Here rest the remains of the Rev. CHARLES A. DAVIDSON, for ten years minister of this parish, who died 15th June 1873 aged 35 years. Also PHOEBE CRUIKSHANK, wife of the above, who died in Hawick 2nd February 1930 aged 91 years.

26a. *Immediately beside Stone 26*
HARRY died 24th April 1870 aged 18 months.

27. Erected to the memory of ALEXANDER McKENZIE, Bareflathills, Elgin, who died at Bareflathills on 22nd June 1903 aged 65. Also his wife ANN NEWLANDS who died at Bareflathills on 20th April 1906 aged 66. Their son JAMES McKENZIE died at Bareflathills on 11th June 1915 aged 43. Their daughter ISABELLA, who died 9th July 1940 aged 71, and their daughter ANNIE who died at Bareflathills on 7th January 1942, aged 80. ALEXANDER McKENZIE, nephew of the foregoing, died at Elgin on 1st January 1943 aged 60.

28. Erected by JOHN McKENZIE, Cart Wright, Calcotts, to the memory of his children JESSIE who died on the 29th day of April 1834 aged 4 years and 6 months, JOHN who died on the 8th day of January 1848 aged 15 years and 9 months.

29. Erected by ANDREW LOGIE, Marchside, Tiendland, in memory of his wife HELEN JAMES who died 12th April 1880 aged 52 years. Also their daughter ISABELLA who died 2nd April 1897 aged 37 years. Also of the said ANDREW LOGIE who died 23rd Novr 1899 aged 74 years.

30. *Two Masons Blocks, both inscribed with*
D.McO.

31. Erected to the memory of MARGARET EDWARDS, beloved wife of JOHN A. KENNEDY, St. Andrews-Lhanbryd Schoolhouse, who died 8th April 1911 aged 26 years. Also of the said JOHN A. KENNEDY M.A. B.Sc., Headmaster St. Andrews-Lhanbryd Public School from 1910 to 1916, and Captain 1/6th Seaforth Highlanders, who died of wounds in France 6th August 1916 aged 37 years. "Dolce et decorum est pro patria mori".

32. *Stone no longer in existence.*

33. *Flat stone*
Heir lies AGNES GEDDES spous to IOHN GRANT in Kirkhill who departed the 20 day of May 1681. I.G., A.G.

34. *Flat stone*
Here lies ane honest woman called CHRISTIAN GEDDES spouse to LENARD BAIRD (…)e(….) who depairted the 13 of September 1676. L.B., C.G.

35. *Flat stone, worn and illegible.*

36. *Stone no longer in existence.*

37. *Stone no longer in existence.*

38. 1887: In memory of JAMES WINCHESTER who died 27 Oct 1877 aged 65 years. And his wife JANE FORBES who died 27 March 1887 aged 72 years. Also their daughters JANE died 24 March 1858 aged 21 years, MARGARET died 4 September 1872 aged 26 years, ELIZABETH died 17 September 1870 aged 21 years.

39. The Leuchars Aisle. The burial enclosure of the Innes Family.
    This enclosure is now totally inaccessible due to the growth of vegetation, and the possibly dangerous state of the walls. The Monumental Inscriptions were recorded by Andrew Jervaise FSA Scot., in his "Epitaphs and Inscriptions in Burial Grounds and on Old Buildings in the North East of Scotland", published in 1875, and they are reproduced here.

39a. Heir lyes ane honorable man ALEXANDER INNES of Mathi Milne who departit November the First 1636.

39b. ALEXANDER INNES. JEAN KINNAIRD – 1688 A.I. I.K.
    The tombstone bears the Innes Coat of Arms.

40. *Flat Stone.*
    Here lies JESPAR WINCHESTER who died in Spynie the 27 of October 1688, also JAMES SIM who died in Pitgavnie May 1658. WILLIAM WINCHESTER his son.
    "Worship Him that made the Heaven the Earth and the Sea and the fountain of water".
    MARGARET SIM his spouse. I.W. M.S.
    "In Memento Mori".

41. In memory of JAMES SMITH died April 1870, his wife MARGARET WILSON died 11th July 1913, their daughters JEANIE died 23rd Jan 1951, ELIZABETH died 17th August 1951, AGNES died 17th Feb 1953, MARY ANN died 10th May 1956.

42. The SANDISON enclosure.
    All traces of the enclosure walls have now been removed.

42a. Sacred to the memory of ANN FINDLAY, the beloved spouse of JAMES SANDISON who died at Woodside, Bareflathills on the 29th March 1857 aged 60 years, much regretted by husband and friends. The said JAMES SANDISON died at Jointure of Leuchars on the 22nd July 1865 aged 68 years.

42b.   In memory of ELIZA JANE REID, wife of ALEXR SANDISON, Loch-Hill, died 19th Sept. 1902 aged 44, also their son JAMES accidentally killed 9th June 1886 aged 12, and their daughter ANNE died in London 20th Decr 1920 aged 37. Also the said ALEXR SANDISON died at Elgin 14th Octr 1936 aged 83 and their son JOHN died at Lhanbryde 22nd June 1951 aged 73 and his wife ANNIE BRANDER died 20th March 1966 aged 83. Also MINNIE SANDISON died 5th June 1978 aged 86.

42c.   *Stone lying flat, face-up.*
Erected by JOHN SANDISON and JESSIE DUNCAN his wife in memory of their beloved children who died at Whitefield, Elgin. WILLIAM who died 25th February 1865 aged 4 years, JAMES who died 5th September 1868 aged 20 years, ANN who died 20th Feb *1870 aged 20 years.* Also the said *JOHN SANDISON who died at Whitefield 2.3.1893* aged 67 years, and his wife JESSIE DUNCAN who died at Elgin 27 February 1897 aged 77 years. Also their daughter WILLIAMINA who died at Elgin 2nd May 1937 aged 79 years.
The section of the inscription reproduced in italics is now missing due to the stone having broken when it fell. This part of the text is taken from an earlier recording, probably ca 1974.

43.   Erected by JAMES BARRY, Shoe maker, Elgin, in memory of his sons WILLIAM who died Jany 21st 1824 aged 13 years and JAS who died Feby 9th 1825 aged 11 years.

44.   Erected by GEORGE ARCHIBALD in memory of his wife BATHIA DEAN who died 4th January 1909 aged 62 years. Also son JAMES who died 21st August 1884 aged 2 years and 3 months. Also son ALEXR who died 25th Sept 1916 aged 43 years, and the above GEORGE ARCHIBALD who died 9th Octr 1917 aged 74 years. Their daughter BATHIA who died 9th January 1935 aged 63 years, also their daughter MARGORY SCOTT who died 26th May 1957 aged 87 years. JANE ARCHIBALD who died 3rd September 1966 aged 82 years. GEORGINA BAIN who died 4th Sept 1981 aged 80 years.

44a   Sacred to the memory of ALEXANDER ARCHIBALD, Urquhart, who died 21st Feby 1868 aged 55 years. His spouse MARJORY WILSON who died 5th Augt 1854 aged 44 years, and their son ALEXANDER who died in infancy, also their son JAMES who died at the Royal Infirmary Edinburgh 30th November 1871 aged 25. Erected by his widow MARGRET SCOTT and his sons GEORGE and JAMES.

45.   Here lie the remains of JAMES GRANT "PUNCHIE" a native of Elgin, who died 2nd July 1873 in the 80th year of his age.
"This monument has been erected by a few gentlemen who respect the memory of Punchie. On his death bed he expressed a wish that he might be laid beside the Lossie and in deference to such request his remains are interred in this spot adjoining the banks of the river he loved so well. Lovers of the

gentle art, on passing, will pause and respect the last resting place of one who was a devoted disciple to the art and who practised it with constant and untiring assiduacity(*sic*) for more than half a century".

JAMES "PUNCHIE" GRANT was a well-known character whose one love in life was fishing, and his favourite spot was on the banks of the River Lossie adjacent to the burial ground in which he now rests.

46. The Gill Enclosure. *The Enclosure walls have now been removed to facilitate maintenance of the cemetery.*

46a. In loving memory of JAMES GILL, Torehead, Pluscarden, who died 11th March 1919 aged 83 years. Also of his sons ALEXANDER GILL, Mains of Edinvale, Dallas, who died at Torehead 13th Augt 1922 aged 43 years. BESSIE YOUNG, wife of the said JAMES GILL who died 24th June 1926 aged 78 years, also son WILLIAM died at Forres 15th Dec. 1952. ELIZABETH GILL, widow of R.J. McGREGOR died at Carden, Hay St., Elgin 18th April 1959 aged 87 years. JESSIE CALDER GILL died at Sanquhar Mains, Forres, 17th July 1959 aged 83 years. ROBERT GILL died at Creator, Northamptonshire 29th March 1969 aged 78 years. ELSIE MORGAN GILL, widow of ROBERT GILL, died at Coventry 28th January 1970 aged 78 years.

46b. In memory of CHARLOTT GILL died at Glasgow 15th Jany 1878 aged 70 years. Also JESSIE CALDER, wife of WILLIAM GILL, Farmer, Rosearie, who died 7th June 1880 aged 82 years, and her husband WILLIAM GILL who died at Maryhill, Boharm, 14th July 1890 aged 82 years.

46c. Here lies interr'd the body of the late ANDREW GILL, Schoolmaster of St. Andrews, who departed this life Sept 5th 1791 aged 66 years.
"He was an affectionate husband, a tender parent, supported the noble character of an honest man, lived much respected, died much lamented by his family and friends".
By ALEXANDER GILL, farmer, Bogton, in memory of his sister MARGARET GILL who died 14th Augt 1827 aged 18 years. His mother JEAN BRANDER who died 23rd November 1844 aged 74 years. His father ALEXANDER GILL who died July 22nd 1851 aged 87 years. His sister JEAN GILL who died December 4th 1869 aged 66 years. Also the said ALEXANDER GILL, Farmer, Bogton, died 27th January 1898 aged 96 years.

47. *Stone no longer in existence.*

48. *This stone was originally within the church of St Andrews, which was demolished in 1796.*
In this church lie interred Mr JOHN PATERSON, once minr of Dipple and 47 years minr of this parish, who died April 20th 1778 in the 81st year of his age and the 51st year of his ministry, and HELEN GRANT his spouse who died January 5th 1769 age 76 years.
"Love to God and charity to men were their prevailing dispositions. He was

fervent in the work of the Gospel, and she was a pious but humble Christian". This monument erected to their memory by their son Mr. ROBERT PATERSON, minr of New Spynie.

49. Erected by WILLIAM STORM, Blacksmith, Elgin, in memory of his sister-in-law ISABELLA STORM who died 22nd January 1877 aged 33 years. Also of his father-in-law DAVID STORM, Tailor, who died 22nd February 1877 aged 66 years.

50. *Stone no longer in existence.*

51. *Stone no longer in existence.*

52. Erected by ALEX McKENZIE in memory of his family: PETER who died in infancy 25th March 1886, MARGARET who died at Aberdeen 24th February 1910 aged 34 years, GEORGE, killed in action in France 9th April 1917 aged 34 years, MARY who died 29th July 1922 aged 32 years, and his wife JESSIE McKENZIE who died March 3rd 1925 aged 80 years. The said ALEX McKENZIE who died 28th September 1934 aged 87 years.

53. Erected by ROBERT MacKENZIE, Tailor, Muir of Corskie, in memory of his wife MARGARET DUNCAN who died 8th December 1866 aged 56 years.

54. *Stone no longer in existence.*

55. …. was erected here by ANDREW FORSYTH, Mason in Elgin, in memory of ISABELLA GEORGE his spouse who died 28th July 1801 aged 30 years, and of JAMES FORSYTH their oldest son who died 26th May 1810 aged 13 years.

56. *Stone no longer in existence.*

57. *Stone no longer in existence.*

58. Erected by JANE and ANNIE GAIR in memory of their father HENRY GAIR who died at St. Andrews 28th Jany 1861 aged 53 years. Also their sister MAGGIE who died 15th April 1855 aged 18 years, and their brother GEORGE who died 8th July 1881 aged 28 years. Also their aunt ISABELLA ROSS who died 24th Novr 1877 aged 67 years, and their mother ANN ROSS who died at Wood Park 15th Novr 1891 aged 82 years. Also the said ANNIE GAIR who died 2nd July 1915 aged 69 years, and JANE GAIR who died 29th August 1915 aged 79 years.
"Blessed are the dead who die in the Lord".

59. *Stone no longer in existence.*

60. Sacred to the memory of their beloved parents ELSPIT BUIE, who died at Greens of Coxton 27th Feby 1861 aged 60 years, also her husband DONALD

McKINZIE who died 20th Novr 1868 aged 64 years.
"Blessed are the dead that die in the Lord, for Jesus is their resurrection".

61. Sacred to the memory of WILLIAM LOGIE who died at Greens of Coxton 9th Jan. 1893, aged 70 years. Also his beloved wife MARGARET McKENZIE who died at Moss of Barmuckity 24th June 1913 aged 73 years.
"Gone but not forgotten".

62. Erected by DONALD McINTOSH, Barmuckity, in memory of his beloved wife ISABELLA GILBERT who died 5th December 1876 aged 45 years. Also their daughters ELIZABETH who died 8th Jany 1877 aged 4 years, and ANN SOPHIA who died 5th March 1878 aged 14 years. ISABELLA died 10th April 1907 aged 41 years. Also the above DONALD McINTOSH died 29th May 1914 aged 85 years.
"Blessed are the dead who die in the Lord".

63. This stone is erected by JAMES NICOL, Farmer, Blackhills, in memory of his wife ANN CAMERON who died on the 5th April 1805 aged 54 years. And their children JOHN and JAMES NICOLS who died of (*sic*) nonage.

64. In loving memory of GEORGE DOUGLAS J.P. of Easter Calcots, born 31st October.1865, died 8th May 1933. Also his wife ELIZABETH FRASER, born 5th April 1862 died 20th April 1942. Also their daughter ANNIE ALEXANDRA GARROW born 25th March 1900, died 17th December 1987 and her husband IAN WILLIAM CRUIKSHANK born 21st May 1898, died 9th October 1961.

65. Erected by R. & J. STEWART, 2, Boath Road, Auldearn, in loving memory of their sons ROBERT, WILLIAM and DEAN who died in infancy. Also the said ROBERT JOHN STEWART died 6th March 1969 aged 74. JESSIE STEWART died 31st March 1969 aged 81.

65a. *Small stone in front of Stone 65.*
In loving memory of our children ROBERT, WILLIAM and DEAN STEWART, died in infancy.

OTHER STONES IDENTIFIED BY
J di FOLCO ca 1965 (PSAS XCIX p211 et seq)

The location of these stones has not been determined.

66. *Flat Stone*
Heir ly... ...the 7 of March 1674 spous to......

67. ..... son who deperted December the 2... 1685.

68. Heir lyis ane honest man calit GEORGE GEDDES, swmtym in dweller in the Walkmylne wha dapairtit the 12 of April 1632 and his spous MARIORI SIMSON who depairtit the 28 Iaiawary 1628.

STONES LOCATED DURING THE BURIED TOMBSTONE RESEARCH PROJECT, 2002.
B.B. Bishop., K.L. Mitchell., H. Mitchell., R Brander., M MacDonald.

These stones were excavated, the tombstones were measured and drawn, and the inscriptions were recorded. Following this the turf was replaced. This is an ongoing research project covering several burial grounds in Morayshire, the results of which will be published in full at a later date.

A. ....lyes the (sp)ouse to IAMES M WINCHER she died the 7 of December 1655. ..... WILLIAM WINCHESTER....."Memento Mori".

B. Here lyes the body of JAMES DUNN who dyed the 18 of Feb 1712 who lived in Todholes. His spoue (*sic*) AGNES GILZEAN and their children. I.D. A.G. I.D. E.R. I.L. "Memento Mori".
This is possibly the Stone 50 noted earlier as now being missing.

C. Here lyes a young man named ROBERT ALSHOUNER, lawfull son to JAMES ALSHOUNER and ISOBEL BRODIE who departed 25 of Agust (*sic*) 1696. I.A. I.B.
"Blessed are the dead which die in the Lord for they rest from their labour and their wor... ... doe follow.... them."

D. ..... THOMSON who deperted December the 2(2) 168(5).
See also stone No 67 above.

E. This stone is placed here in memory of WILIAM HAY, late Miller in Leuchars who died 3 Jany 18101 (*sic*) aged 77 years and his spouse JANNET BROWN who died 6th April 1802 aged 57.
This is possibly the Stone 56 noted earlier as now being missing.

F. Hic Requisumt Reliyium Um Admodium pij & Reverendi domini GAVIN WITHERSPOON insgentissimi quondam Ecclesiae sideris fidelis proeconus Magistriorum verbi Divini qui Clarissimum testimonium Conte temporis hu Defectiones per subuit & Cum quatuordec Annos Diliogenta issimus suisset Pastor Evangelicus in hac Paroch quinquagesimo & sexto olectis suo Anno Vitam terrestram Cotelli *Comunitat* Decessit huic Mundo Martij 26 1715. Silius est huimli CLARUS WITHERSPOONUS Hebelis heu Canctis ...*adit ille probes precious Referns heri mysteria docuit populum sedulous sy*....
The stone has been transcribed exactly as engraved, the areas in italics are badly worn.

MONUMENTAL INSCRIPTIONS

BLACKHILLS HOUSE

PARISH OF ELGIN

B/1. AMY CHRISTIE daughter of ROBERT CHRISTIE C.A. Edinburgh, born 4th May 1855, died 26th November 1931. THOMAS NORTH CHRISTIE, formerly a member of The Legislative Council of Ceylon, born 12th September 1852, died 7th January 1939. ROSE CHRISTIE, their sister, born 5th May 1859, died 18th April 1953. SYLVESTER FALCONER CHRISTIE of Blackhills, their nephew, born 26th May 1914, died 13th June 1983, and his wife GEORGINA, born 10th January 1921, died 14th March 1984.

The Christie Tombstone at Blackhills

INDEX

Alexander	23	Gilbert	62
Alshouner	C	Gill	46a, 46b, 46c
Anderson	4, 7, 13	Gilzean	22, B
Archibald	44, 44a	Gordon	20
Asher	22	Grant	5b, 9, 33, 45, 48
Bain	44	Hay	6b, 8, E
Baird	34	Hendry	11
Barnet	2		
Barry	43	Innes	2, 39a, 39b
Bennett	1		
Brander	5b, 5c, 42b, 46c	James	29
Brodie	C	Jamieson	7
Brown	E	Johnston	21
Buie	60		
		Keith	7
Calder	46a, 46b	Kennedy	31
Cameron	14, 63	Kinnaird	39b
Chalmers	14		
Christie	B/1	Lamb	8
Cranna	7	Leal	15
Cruikshank	26, 64	Legge	6b
		Leslie	25
Davidson	26	Logie	29, 61
Dean	44		
Douglas	64	McArthur	10
Duff	20	M(a)cDonald	1, 9, 19
Dunbar	5b, 5c, 13	McGregor	46a
Dunbar-Brander	5a, 5b, 5c	McIntosh	62
Duncan	10, 24, 42c, 53	M(a)cKenzie	11, 24a, 27, 28
Dunn	B		52, 53, 61
		McKinzie	60
Edwards	31	M(a)cLean	21
		Mitchell	13
Falconer	18, B/1	Morgan	6a, 6b,
Farquhar	19		
Ferguson	23, 24a	Newlands	27
Findlay	42a	Nicholson	4
Forbes	38	Nicol	63
Forsyth	55	North	B/1
Fraser	2, 25, 64		
		Paterson	6a, 6b, 48
Gair	58	Petrie	22
Garrow	64	Priest	11
Geddes	33, 34, 68		
George	55	Reid	42b

13

Ross	58
Sandison	42a, 42b, 42c
Scott	44, 44a
Sellar	7
Sim	40
Sim(p)son	23, 68
Smith	13, 41
Souter	7
Stephen	7
Stewart	65, 65a
Storm	49
Thom(p)son	5a, D
Torrance	16
Walker	20
Wilson	41, 44a
Wincher	A
Winchester	38, 40, A
Witherspoon(us)	F
Wright	13
Young	46a

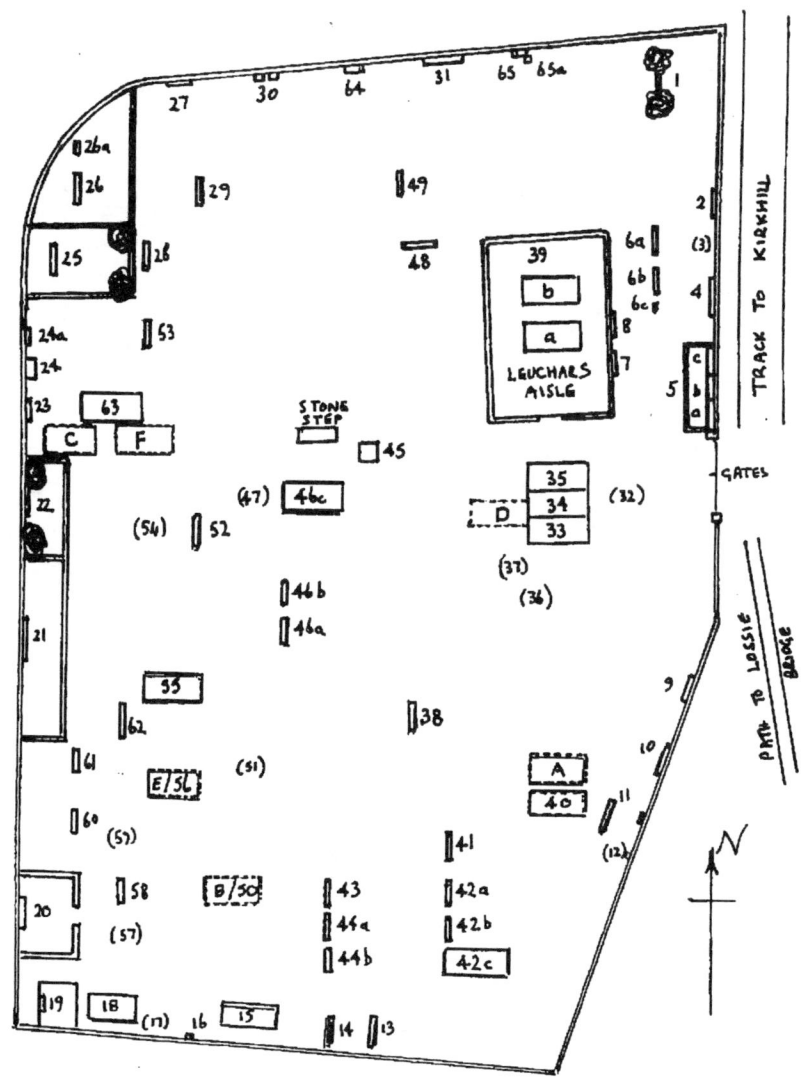

Plan of the Burial Ground at Kirkhill, September 2002

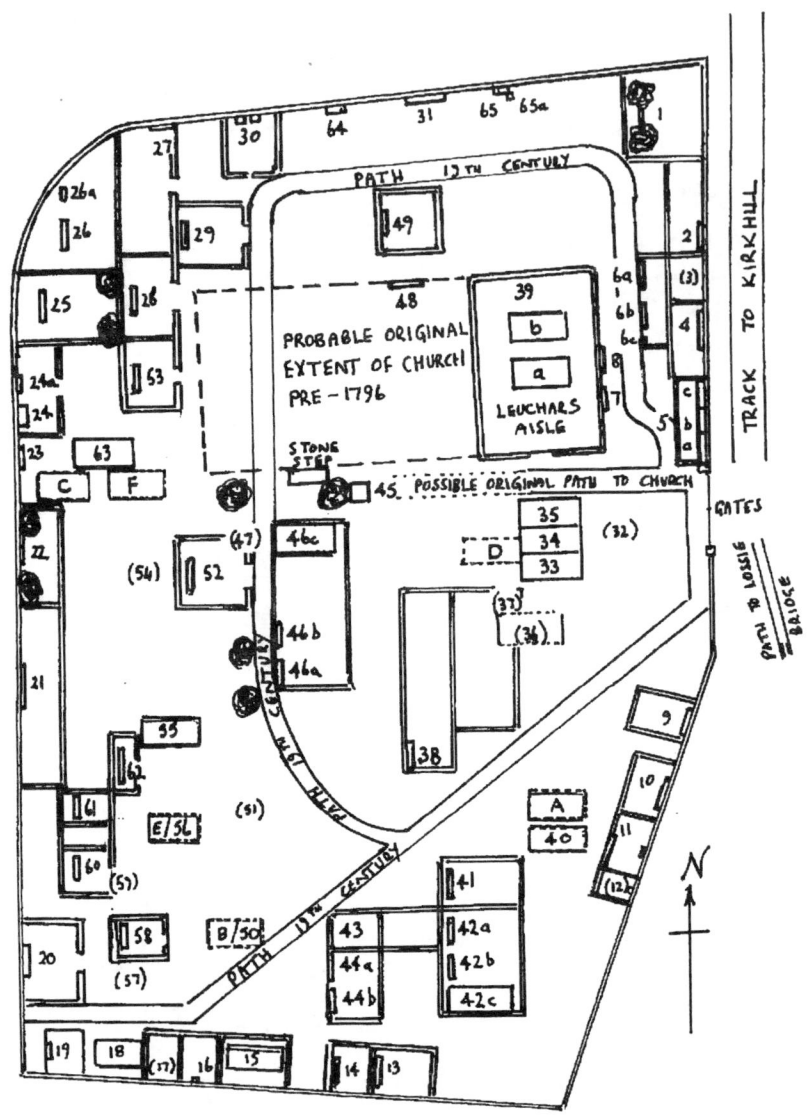

Plan of the Burial Ground at Kirkhill, showing site of pre-1796 church, 19th century pathways, and enclosures which were removed mid-20th century